The Wayland Library of Science and Technology

ORIGINS OF LIFE

CLINT TWIST

The Wayland Library of Science and Technology

The Nature of Matter
The Universal Forces
Stars and Galaxies
The Solar System
The Changing Landscape
Air and Oceans
Origins of Life
The Science of Life
Plants and Animals
Animal Behaviour
The Human Machine
Health and Medicine

The Environment
Feeding the World
Raw Materials
Manufacturing Industry
Energy Sources
The Power Generators
Transport
Space Travel
Communications
The Computer Age
Scientific Instruments
Towards Tomorrow

Advisory Series Editor
Robin Kerrod

Consultants
Professor D.C. Imrie, Dr P. Whitfield

Editor: Steve Luck
Designer: David West · Children's Book Design
Production: Steve Elliott
Director: John Ridgeway
Project Director: Lawrence Clarke

First published in 1990 by
Wayland (Publishers) Ltd
61 Western Road, Hove
East Sussex BN3 1JD, England

AN EQUINOX BOOK

Planned and produced by:
Equinox (Oxford) Limited
Musterlin House, Jordan Hill Road,
Oxford OX2 8DP

Nel 5.93 17 08

Copyright © Equinox (Oxford) Ltd 1990

British Library Cataloguing in Publication Data
Twist, Clint
Origins of Life
1. Organisms, Evolution
I. Title
575

ISBN 1-85210-891-6

- Evol.
- Man, - Origin
- Prehistoric man

Media conversion and typesetting by Peter
MacDonald, Una Macnamara and Vanessa Hersey
Origination by Hong Kong Reprohouse Co Ltd
Printed in Italy by Rotolito Lombarda
S.p.A., Milan
Bound in France by AGM

Front cover: Fossil ammonites in a sample
of rock over 172 million years old.
Back cover: *Triceratops*, the largest horned
dinosaur.

Contents

Introduction

Human beings are among the most recent of the
animal species that now inhabit the Earth. Our
early ancestors did not appear until about 3 million
years ago. But the first traces of life appeared on
Earth over 3,000 million years ago. Life seemed to
have begun in the oceans, and there it stayed until
about 400 million years ago. Then life moved to
the land and began to diversify and thrive as
never before.

We can trace the gradual development, or
evolution, of living things through their remains,
or fossils, in the rocks. Species have come and gone
over the ages as the Earth's climate and surface
have changed. Those better suited to the new
conditions would tend to survive, while others
would perish. This idea of the survival of the fittest
is a cornerstone of one of the greatest scientific
theories, the theory of evolution.

◄ Fossil ammonites in a sample of
rock over 172 million years old.
Ammonites were shelled creatures
that lived at the time of the dinosaurs.
They became extinct at the
same time, 65 million years ago.

Origins of life

Our planet was formed about 4,600 million years ago. Some time during the first 1,000 million years, life in its most basic form appeared on Earth. There is a theory that the Earth might have been "infected" with life from outer space. But life was probably created from simple chemicals that occurred in the early Earth's atmosphere and in the oceans. Gradually, natural chemistry produced more complex substances that became the building blocks of life. For the next 3,000 million years, life was confined to the seas, where it began. Traces of early lifeforms can be found as fossils embedded in rock.

Fossils

Fossils are the remains of animals and plants that over millions of years have been converted into stone. They are evidence of early life on Earth, and are usually found embedded in other rocks. Fossils range from faint traces and footprints, to complete plants and animals, showing details of size and shape.

When a living thing dies, it does not always decay. Sometimes it is covered with layers of mud, which gradually turn into rock. The structure of the plant or animal also turns to stone and is preserved as a fossil. Much of what we know about the evolution of life and prehistoric plants and animals comes from the study of fossils.

The oldest fossils

In the 1950s fossil hunters began finding evidence of the first living things. Microscopic fossil bacteria have been found in rocks dating from more than 3,000 million years ago. The oldest fossils visible to the naked eye are about 1,800 million years old. They are the remains of stromatolites, structures built up by colonies of millions of single-celled plants.

▲ A cross-section through a fossil stromatolite shows how millions of single-celled plants were organized in layers to form a colony.

▼ Structures similar to fossil stromatolites are still being formed in warm, shallow seawater. For example, they can be seen as large lumps, covered in seaweed, at low tide on the coast of South Africa.

Dawn of life

For 1,000 million years, chemical reactions in the world's ancient oceans produced a thin "soup" of complex organic chemicals. As the soup simmered on hot rocks at the edges of the seas, cells developed that were able to reproduce themselves. These earliest cells are known as prokaryotes.

About 2,500 million years ago, one group of prokaryotes became able to use the energy of sunlight to make food. This was the beginning of photosynthesis. These cells eventually became the first primitive green plants. Prokaryotes still exist today as bacteria and the closely related blue-green algae.

The first complex cells
Early simple cells gradually developed into more complex ones. Prokaryotes started forming communities of cells, such as those forming stromatolites. But the great leap forward came about 1,200 million years ago, with the appearance of cells with a nucleus. The nucleus is a central core that controls the cell's activities. These more complex cells are called eukaryotes. They gave rise to the great diversity of life on Earth. The first eukaryotes were probably simple plants and tiny single-celled animals called protozoa.

▶ Life in the early oceans. Jellyfish (1) and burrowing worms (5) look much the same as their present-day descendants. The two species that are anchored to the sea bed (2 and 4) resemble modern sea-pens, a form of soft coral. The circular worms (6) and the strange disc-shaped creature (3) are unlike any known animals. They must have either died out or evolved into something else. None was very big. The worms were about 2 cm long, and the sea-pens may have grown 12 cm tall.

Invertebrate fossils

1 *Cyclops medusa*	4 *Charnodiscus*
2 *Glaessnerina*	5 A burrowing worm
3 *Dickinsonia*	6 *Tribrachidium*

◀ The earliest animals have left only faint traces. The fossil worm tracks (left) are clearly identifiable, but tell us practically nothing about the worm. The "mould" of an external surface (right) shows that the animal was made up of segments.

Multi-celled life

The first animals and plants that consisted of many cells appeared about 1,000 million years ago. The first animals were small and had few hard parts. For this reason, they did not readily form fossils and so they have left very little trace of their existence.

Some of the earliest fossils are the tracks and tunnels made by soft-bodied worms at the bottom of the sea. All the available evidence strongly suggests that by about 680 million years ago, there were already many different forms of life, concentrated in shallow seas. They were poised for the next evolutionary step, the development of hard skins and shells that provided outer protection.

▲ A fossil sea-pen. The animal resembled a feather, growing out of the seabed. Not until animals developed hard shells do fossils become more informative.

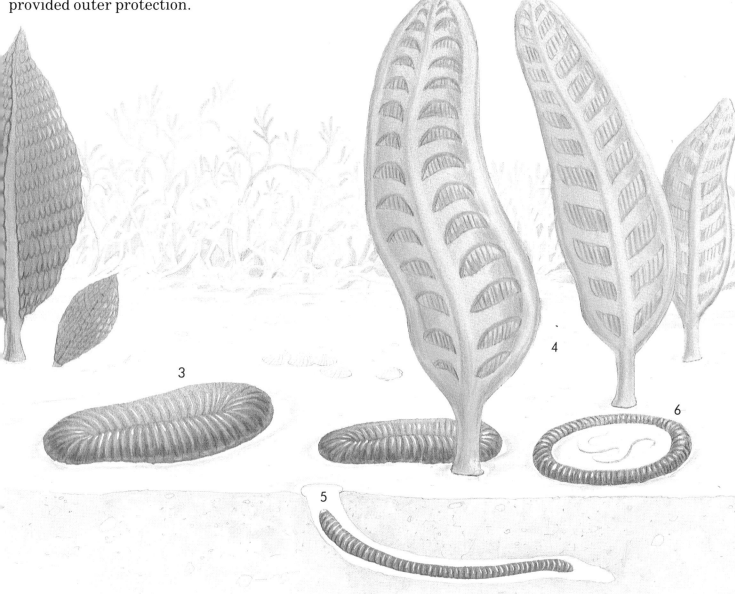

3

4

6

5

Record in the rocks

Fossils in the rocks tell the story of the development of life on Earth. We can read the story in the correct order because the rocks started as layer upon layer of mud and other sediments on the bottom of ancient seas. Each layer took millions of years to form, and they are often thousands of metres thick and very deep down. Only in a very few places are rocks older than 600 million years near enough to the surface for us to find fossils in them.

The study of fossils is called palaeontology. This science first began as a branch of geology, the study of the Earth. Then biologists began to become interested in fossils to date stages of evolution. If a fossil is found in a rock of a certain age, that must also be the age of the fossil.

Imperfect record

The fossil record is far from perfect, and new discoveries are being made every year. Fossils are found only when rocks are exposed at the surface, or during mining and tunnelling. The folding and movement of the rock layers, and the action of rivers and earthquakes, have exposed areas of rock from all periods of the Earth's history.

Some rocks provide better fossils than others. Rocks are made up of tiny particles called grains. Fine-grained rocks, such as slate and limestone, provide much better quality fossils than coarse-grained rocks, such as sandstone. From fairly recent times we have some almost perfect specimens that have been preserved in drops of amber (fossil resin from trees) and natural deposits of tar.

Fossils provide a wide range of information. The discovery of a number of different species in the same small area of rock helps us to form a picture of the community of life at that time. Fossils can be used to trace how a species has developed over hundreds of millions of years. The fossil record also has remains of species that no longer exist. Scientists use such fossils to work out what the creatures looked like.

◀ This near-perfect fossil skull of a sabre-toothed tiger is about 2 million years old. Scientists can take accurate measurements from such well-preserved specimens and compare them with modern species.

▼ Ammonites are one of the most common fossils, and there are hundreds of different varieties. They flourished in the oceans for more than 300 million years, then suddenly vanished from the fossil record.

Cross-section of rocks

The Grand Canyon provides spectacular scenery, and a slice through geological time. The Colorado River has slowly cut down through 1,500 million years of rock layers. The present topmost layer consists of Permian rock about 250 million years old. A little way down the Canyon side are fossilized sea creatures that lived 300 million years ago. Lower down, there are fossil shellfish from 500 million years ago. At the bottom are rocks dating from about 1,700 million years ago.

Geological timescale

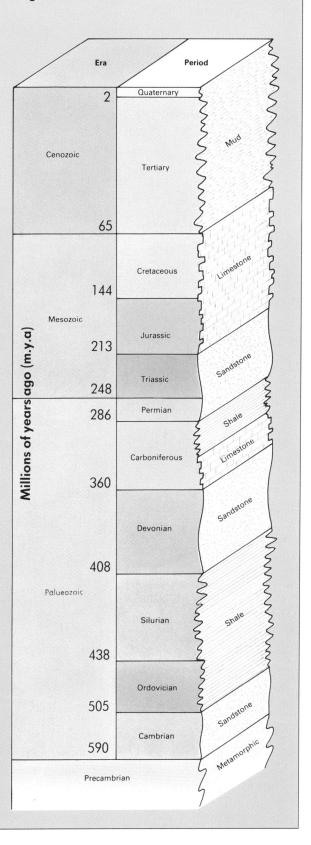

Explosion of life

Once animal life became established in the seas, it developed very rapidly. Different animal groups pioneered each new development: jointed legs, eyes, claws and backbones. About 395 million years ago came a great breakthrough: life moved on to the land. By this time many animals had reached their present-day forms. But life kept on developing. The first four-legged animals, the amphibians, gave rise to a new group – the reptiles. Today, there are still a few amphibian species, such as frogs, and various reptiles, like snakes and lizards. But the most highly evolved animals are the mammals.

▶ A prehistoric footprint. Some of the most dramatic fossils ever found are dinosaur footprints, formed in mud and then preserved as rock for more than 80 million years.

The Cambrian

The Cambrian Period (590-505 million years ago) saw the establishment of early forms of most present-day invertebrates, the animals that have no backbones. Animals resembling sponges and worms lived on the seabed. But the pace of development was set by the trilobites. These were among the first arthropods, animals with jointed limbs, like crabs and insects. They were also the first animals to develop really efficient eyes.

Arthropods are thought to have evolved from worms which developed a pair of legs on each of the many segments that made up their bodies. The earliest ones still look like worms. The trilobites looked rather like woodlice, although there were thousands of different species. They were highly mobile herbivores (plant-eaters),

and they dominated the Cambrian seas. The trilobite "design" was very successful, but it had its limitations. Other arthropods developed specialized limbs that could be used for grasping and grabbing. This enabled them to tackle different foods.

The first meat-eaters

The other widespread animals in the Cambrian seas were the brachiopods. They were a kind of armoured worm, resembling a present-day shellfish. Towards the end of the period there was a very noticeable increase in the number of fleshy animals with hard shells. The shells acted as protective armour. This was a necessary defence against the first carnivores, or meat-eating animals.

Key
1 Brachiopod
2 Trilobites
3,4,5 Arthropods
6 Sea lily (crinoid)
7 Sponge
8 Sea anemones

▼ Trilobites and brachiopods make up 90 per cent of Cambrian fossils, but many other lifeforms flourished. All the animals shown here shared the same habitat about 550 million years ago. The trilobites display their characteristic shape, and the smaller arthropods are developing primitive claws. The sponge, sea anemone, and sea lily have already acquired their basic present-day shape.

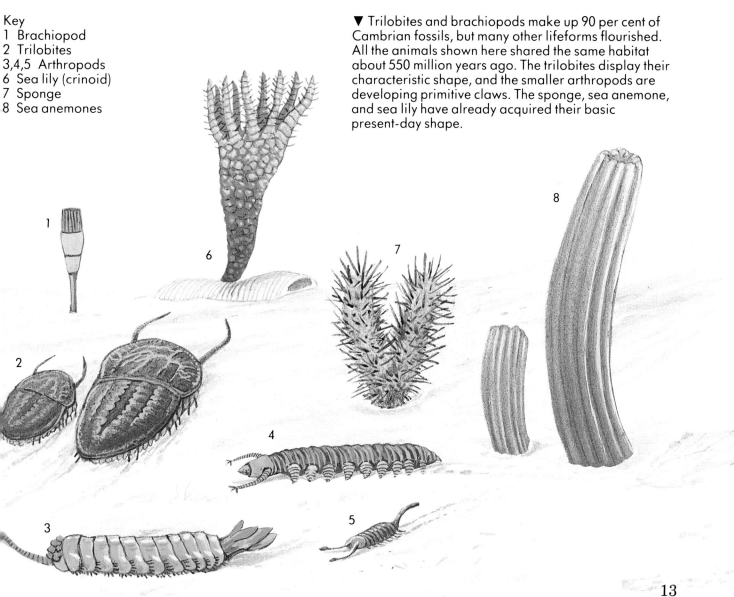

13

The Ordovician

During the Ordovician Period (505-438 million years ago), invertebrates continued to develop. Many gained their present-day characteristics. The headless animals, such as starfish and sea urchins, began to populate the seabed in large numbers. And sponges, corals, sea cucumbers and molluscs all developed their basic shapes and flourished. Towards the end of the period, the first sea-scorpions emerged. Their well-developed pincers, positioned in front of the mouth, made them much more efficient than the trilobites at gathering food. They became underwater hunters.

Into deeper water

Animal life slowly began to extend out of the shallowest water, as first brown and then red algae (seaweed) moved progressively deeper. Around the beginning of the period, tiny, half-worm, half-fish creatures called lancelets appeared. They had a kind of spine called a notochord. The notochord marks the beginning of the development of the spinal chord and the backbone. By the middle of the Ordovician Period, the first primitive fish had evolved. These were small creatures 5-8 cm long, which fed by sucking in water and filtering out tiny animals and plants. They are generally considered to be the first vertebrates (animals with a backbone). The spine of such fish was very weak; for support they had instead a tough skin consisting of interlocking plates, which acted like a suit of armour.

▼ A fossil trilobite. Trilobites flourished for more than 200 million years and were one of the most successful groups of animals of all time. They were arthropods that lived on the seabed. A few were swimmers, and some burrowed into the mud. The spines gave an increased area without adding much weight. Trilobites became extinct about 300 million years ago.

The Silurian

Salt and freshwater fish

The Silurian Period (438-408 million years ago) was a time when life swarmed in the shallow seas. Corals built up huge reefs, providing a place for many types of invertebrates to live. During a relatively short span of time (45 million years) two major animal types – the fish and the arthropods – made great progress in their development.

Jawless fish, which fed by sucking in their food, gradually invaded freshwater rivers and lakes. In these quiet inland backwaters, the first fish with jaws evolved. These were also the first that fed on other fish, and they remained confined to fresh water. A little later in the sea, fish called placoderms appeared. They were covered in hard, bony plates. Ranging in size from a few centimetres up to 9 m in length, they were powerful predators.

Scorpions on the move

On the sea bottom, sea-scorpions were evolving rapidly. The development of grasping claws gave them a strong advantage as predators. Some also developed strong paddles for swimming. One species was more than 2 m long.

◀ ▼ The fossil shellfish on the left has been magnified 700 times to show its intricate internal structure. Countless billions of such tiny animals lived in the ancient seas. Over millions of years their minute skeletons formed thick layers of sediment on the seabed which gradually turned into rock. The cliffs in the picture below are made of such rocks.

▼ Layers of sediment on the sea bottom form bands of rock called strata, such as these layers of chalk and clay. (The coin is there to show scale). Under a microscope we can see thousands of tiny fossils in such rock.

The Devonian

At the very end of the Silurian Period (about 408 million years ago) both plants and animals first made the great transition from water to land. Some of the first land plants with a system for transporting water inside their structure had stems, but neither roots nor leaves. The first air-breathing animals were almost certainly small scorpions. Their legs and claws gave them the mobility that was needed to catch prey in the new environment.

The Devonian Period (408-360 million years ago) is sometimes called the Age of Fishes. The new kinds of fish included the sharks, with their cartilage skeletons, and the bony fishes. All had very strong backbones. By the end of the period they had taken over from the earlier types. There were two kinds of fish with bony skeletons. One kind (called ray-finned) had ordinary fins, and the other (bony-finned) had bones that extended into their fins.

Many forms of sea-life have been excellently preserved as fossils. The strong shells of the brachiopods (1) are easily identifiable, as is the typical shape of the sea lily (2). The long tapering internal skeleton of the squid (3) is more of a puzzle, because the soft body shape and tentacles have not been preserved. On the fossil of a fish (4) even individual scales can be seen.

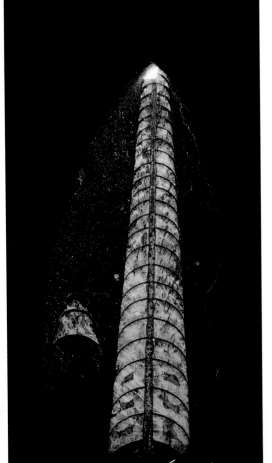

All the descendants of the sharks and ray-finned fish have remained in the sea. But some of the bony-finned fish, which lived in the shallowest water, began to develop the ability to breathe air. At the same time, their fins became more muscular, enabling them to scramble about on land. These fish are now extinct. But during the Devonian Period, some of them evolved into new, four-legged creatures that breathed air. These were the amphibians.

Land plants had by now developed into large tubular structures that were efficient at sucking moisture from the soil. The first swampy forests appeared, full of giant horsetails and ferns. These forests were home to the first wingless insects, the springtails and bristletails. The first millipedes and spiders also appeared. By the middle of the period, the arthropods had established themselves as the dominant land animals.

Late Devonian lakeside

Amphibians were the first vertebrates to walk on dry land. They were also the first four-legged animals. *Icthyostega* (below) was one of the first true amphibians, although fossils reveal that its tail was still rather fish-like. The legs, which had evolved from the fish's bony fins, were well developed. This shows that it probably spent most of its time on land. The adults were about 1 m long, and probably fed on insects. On land they had nothing to fear except the scorpions, which by this time had developed a powerful sting in their tails. Like all amphibians, *Icthyostega* had to return to the water in order to lay its soft-shelled eggs. These were probably rather like frogspawn, and hatched into tadpole-like creatures.

The Carboniferous

Huge swampy forests and jungles covered the Earth during the Carboniferous Period (360-286 million years ago, or m.y.a.). The ground lay thick with rotting vegetation that was later to become coal. Insects had taken to the air by this time and many different species of cockroaches and centipedes had also appeared. But above all this was the Age of Amphibians, which were ideally suited to the damp conditions. Those that spent most of their time out of the water had strong, muscular legs. Some of the later species grew as big as alligators.

The Permian Period (286-248 m.y.a.)
During this period, some of the amphibians developed the ability to lay hard-skinned eggs, which could survive on land without drying out. These were the first reptiles, but only just. Their fossils are often almost identical to true amphibian fossils. By the end of the period many different reptiles had appeared, and had colonized the dry land away from water. Then suddenly about half of all animal species became extinct. Sea-scorpions and trilobites disappeared from the seas. Most large amphibians and many of the early reptiles also died out. These extinctions mark the end of the Palaeozoic Era, the time of primitive life.

The Triassic Period (248-213 m.y.a.)
A new group of animals, the dinosaurs, emerged from the disaster. At first quite small, the dinosaurs rapidly developed a wide variety of shapes and sizes during this period. The first lizards, tortoises and crocodiles also appeared around this time. Another group of reptiles developed some of the characteristics of mammals. Some were warm-blooded and suckled their young. The first true mammals, tiny insect-eaters the size of shrews, also appear for the first time as Triassic fossils.

▶ The forests of the Carboniferous Period were dominated by huge primitive conifers (1), club mosses (2, 6) and horsetail creepers (4) climbing up around the tree-trunks. The undergrowth was a tangle of tree ferns (3), horsetails (10) and club-moss roots (5). Dragonflies (7) flitted through the damp air, and the vegetation provided food for centipedes (9). Many amphibians (11) grew quite large. Those that stayed in the water (8) had a much more eel-like appearance.

18

The Jurassic

The Jurassic Period (213-144 million years ago) was the height of the Mesozoic Era, the time of middle life. The mammal-like reptiles soon became extinct and the dinosaurs and true reptiles took over. Some dinosaurs were the largest land animals that ever lived, and some were no bigger than a large hen. For 100 million years, on land, in the air and in the water, these animals ruled the Earth. Herds of large and small herbivores, some armoured, some not, grazed the vegetation. The largest dinosaurs weighed 80 tonnes and stood over 20 m tall. They evolved long necks in order to reach the highest leaves.

Other species developed into ferocious carnivores with sharp fangs and teeth. Huge flying lizards preyed on their smaller relatives, some of which were gradually evolving into primitive birds. At sea, the icthyosaurs (fish-lizards) bore a remarkable resemblance to the modern dolphin. The insects also increased in variety at this time. Bees, wasps, ants and flies all evolved during the Jurassic Period. Fossils show that mammals were still very small.

The Cretaceous Period (144-65 m.y.a.)

During this period, the dinosaurs reached the height of their evolution. Many had become fairly lightweight, fast-running species. Others had evolved into tank-like armoured giants, or ferocious flesh-eaters like *Tyrannosaurus*. But other life was also evolving. Snakes, birds, flowering plants and trees all emerged in their present forms at around this time. Mammals were also developing noticeably, using different methods of reproducing instead of laying eggs. Then suddenly there was another catastrophe of some kind, and dinosaurs died out. The death of the dinosaurs marks the end of the Mesozoic Era, and the beginning of modern life.

▶ *Rhamphorhynchus* (1) soared high above the Jurassic landscape. On the ground, herbivores fed on the foliage of conifers and ginkgoes (2). The largest, such as *Brachiosaurus* (3), had little to fear. Their smaller relatives, such as *Dicraeosaurus* (4), fled into shallow water at the approach of a predator like *Megalosaurus* (5), only to be threatened by crocodiles (9). Stegosaurs (6) were protected by spiky armour while they grazed on ferns and horsetails (10,11). Smaller dinosaurs (7, 8) relied on speed to escape.

The Tertiary

The Tertiary Period (65-2 million years ago) was the beginning of the Cenozoic Era, the time of modern life. It was marked by a tremendous increase in the different kinds of mammals.

Nearly all modern mammal species started as small rabbit-sized creatures. Rodents, such as rats, appeared about 50 million years ago. Bats, primates and whales developed about 10 million years later. By about 30 million years ago, cats, dogs, horses and pigs had joined the growing ranks of mammals.

Between 26 and 27 million years ago, mammal life reached its greatest ever diversity. There were thousands of variations on present-day types. The largest land mammal ever, a giant rhinoceros more than 6 m tall, lived about 20 million years ago.

During the later part of the Tertiary Period, the great continents finally achieved their present shapes. But because of lower sea levels, there were land bridges between continents – for instance, between Asia and North America. Mammals that had evolved in one part of the world could now begin a series of great migrations. Elephants spread from Africa to America and Eurasia; pigs and cats moved in the opposite direction. By the end of the Tertiary Period, all life on Earth had evolved its basic present-day forms.

The Quaternary Period (2 m.y.a. – today)

During the most recent geological period, many other mammals grew to enormous size compared with their modern descendants. There were giant deer with antlers 3 m across. During this period there were several ice ages, when temperatures were much colder than normal. By the end of the last ice age, about 10,000 years ago, all the giant mammals – except whales – had died out. Life on Earth was much the same as we see it today.

▶ By the last part of the Tertiary Period, deciduous trees and flowering plants had spread throughout the Earth. In this African scene, ancestors of the elephant *Amebeledon* (1) and camel *Procamelus* (2), share a waterhole. In the background ancestors of the horse gallop across the plains. *Neohipparion* (3) had three toes, and had not yet developed proper hooves. *Pliohippus* (4) was the first of the one-toed horses.

The human ape

Spot facts

Spot facts

• *The oldest human fossils are of a young woman who has been named Lucy; she lived over 3 million years ago.*

• *The first industries developed about 1½ million years ago, when primitive people began making stone axes.*

• *The "cave-men" used caves for shelter, but most people probably lived in tents or wooden shelters.*

• *Neanderthal people were far from stupid. Their brains were actually bigger than the modern human brain. Nobody knows why the Neanderthals disappeared about 35,000 years ago.*

▶ These footprints clearly preserved in stone show that two adults and a child once walked across a muddy area of Africa about 4 million years ago. The way the footprints are placed tells us that by this time our distant ancestors walked upright.

The story of humans is both fascinating and incomplete. Many parts of the story are known, but there is a large gap in the fossil record during a critical stage of our development. Our closest living relatives are the apes. However, we are a very special kind of ape. We have learnt how to speak, and how to make and use tools. Since humans first walked out of Africa about 1 million years ago, we have spread to every part of the world, and adapted to many of its environments.

Our ancestors

▼ Skulls are the most durable of hominid remains. They enable us to measure the size of the brain. We can trace our ancestry through the development of the skull.

Family tree

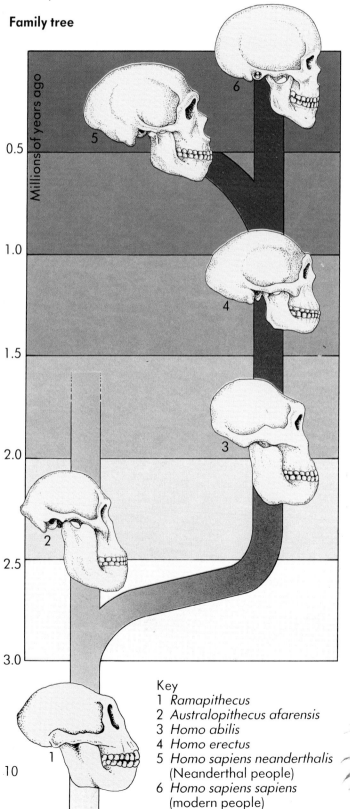

Millions of years ago

0.5

1.0

1.5

2.0

2.5

3.0

10

Key
1 *Ramapithecus*
2 *Australopithecus afarensis*
3 *Homo abilis*
4 *Homo erectus*
5 *Homo sapiens neanderthalis*
(Neanderthal people)
6 *Homo sapiens sapiens*
(modern people)

Fossils tell us that between 14 and 8 million years ago a type of ape called *Ramapithecus* was widespread from present-day France to northern India. The first *Ramapithecus* fossil was discovered in northern India in 1932.

Ramapithecus was probably the first relative of the hominids, human-like apes. It probably lived in partially wooded regions and spent a lot of its time on the ground. It may have left the trees altogether. All of its weight would certainly have been on its back legs while feeding. This would have freed its hands to gather more food such as roots, nuts and seeds. When walking any distance, however, *Ramapithecus* almost certainly used all four limbs, rather like a modern chimpanzee. No hominid fossils have been found dating from the 4-million-year period following the disappearance of *Ramapithecus*.

▼ *Ramapithecus* was very ape-like in appearance. Collecting food on the ground, and not in the trees, probably encouraged the habit of walking upright.

Early people

About 4 million years ago, parts of what is now eastern Africa were inhabited by small hominids who walked upright all the time. These are our earliest direct ancestors. We have no fossil remains of them, but we know that they developed into two subgroups. One of these groups is called *Australopithecus*. The earliest fossil hominid is of a female, whose bones are 3.2 million years old. She was discovered in Ethiopia by an American scientist, John Johanson, in 1974, and named Lucy.

By about 2.5 million years ago, two distinct kinds of *Australopithecus* had emerged. One was larger and stronger, and is called the robust type. The other was more slender. It is called the gracile type. Both probably carried sticks and threw stones. But no tools have ever been found with their remains. All types of *Australopithecus* became extinct about 1 million years ago.

Nothing is known about the other side of Lucy's family tree until around 2.5 million years ago, when the first true human appeared. The earliest type is known as *Homo habilis* "skilful man". The earliest fossil remains of *Homo habilis* coincide with the first real tools – crudely shaped pieces of stone. Big stones were used for smashing up animal bones to get at the marrow, and sharp flakes of rock were used to cut up the meat.

About 1.5 million years ago the next type of human emerged, *Homo erectus* "erect man". They were able to make better tools, by chipping stones into cutting tools called hand-axes. Groups of *Homo erectus* in different areas of Africa developed different techniques of making stone tools. By about 1 million years ago, *Homo erectus* had learned to make use of fire, and had invented cooking. At about that time, they began to spread out from Africa.

H. afarensis

▼ Lucy belonged to the earliest type of *Australopithecus*, which is known as *afarensis*. Her brain was only about a quarter the size of a modern human's. Although her descendants grew taller and stronger, their brains remained about the same size and they never learned to make tools.

▶ The brain of *Homo habilis* was about half the size of that of modern people but was twice as large as that of *Australopithecus*. This increase in brain power enabled *Homo habilis* to learn how to make the first crude stone tools, which could be used to cut up dead animals.

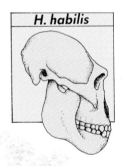

H. habilis

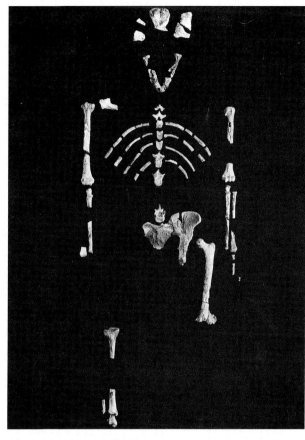

An apewoman called Lucy

Lucy is the nickname of the fossil of a female *Australopithecus*. By studying the knee and hip joints scientists are certain it was a female who walked upright like a modern human. She was 1.2 m tall and died at about 23 years old.

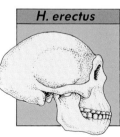

H. erectus

▶ *Homo erectus* had a brain about two-thirds modern size. The increase in brain size over *Homo habilis* was quite small. However, it was enough to enable *Homo erectus* to develop quite sophisticated stone tools, and to learn how to make and use fire. Once *Homo erectus* had fire, they moved north to cooler climates, using the discovery to keep warm.

Prehistoric people

We know from fossils that *Homo erectus* had spread into Europe and the Far East by around 500,000 years ago. By this time these early humans had learned to make semi-permanent campsites where the hunting was good. The examination of an early European campsite (made about 400,000 years ago) has shown that rhinoceroses were the most common prey. Presumably, this was because they provided plenty of meat. Beavers were also hunted in large numbers for their warm fur.

Over the next 200,000 years, *Homo erectus* slowly evolved into *Homo sapiens* "wise man". By about 200,000 years ago, the transformation from one group to the other was complete, but human evolution was not quite finished. Two further subgroups developed: *Homo sapiens sapiens* "modern man" and Neanderthal people.

These were the so-called "cave-men", but the term is misleading. Both groups used caves to shelter from the cold of the ice age and from dangerous animals, such as the sabre-toothed tiger. But both groups also made tents and wooden shelters, and inhabited grassland and forests. The reason these prehistoric people are associated with caves is that the best-preserved evidence of human occupation has been found in caves. In the same way, stone tools are the only ones to survive. But prehistoric people undoubtedly made baskets and nets, which have long since crumbled into dust.

Neanderthal people first appeared in Europe about 120,000 years ago. They are often said to be stupid and beast-like, but nothing is further from the truth. The Neanderthals were skilled stoneworkers, and are the first people known to have buried their dead. In one grave that was discovered recently, a bunch of flowers had been placed with the body.

Homo sapiens sapiens first appeared in southern Africa about 100,000 years ago, and these people quickly developed the skills that would make them the masters of the planet. Their stone tools became increasingly more specialized and finely crafted. By the time they moved northwards about 40,000 years ago, they had learned how to carve bone and ivory into spearheads, needles and combs.

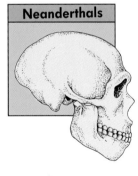

Neanderthals

▼ The brain of the Neanderthals was larger than that of modern people. Around 35,000 years ago Neanderthals died out and we do not know why. Some scientists have suggested they were killed off by *Homo sapiens sapiens*, but this seems unlikely.

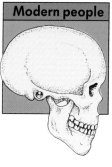

Modern people

▲ A painting of a bison on the roof of the cave of Altamira, in the Pyrenees Mountains in Spain. It is a superb example of prehistoric art. The earliest European cave paintings date from around 20,000 years ago, and depict the animals that were hunted by prehistoric people. They may have been painted for religious or magical reasons.

► Tents made of animal skins were a much more practical form of shelter than caves. They could be packed up and carried if the animal herds that were hunted for food moved away.

▼ These prehistoric implements range from crudely shaped hand-axes to finely formed arrowheads.

The human race

Human migration from southern Africa began at least 50,000 years ago. Towards the end of the last ice age, about 20,000 years ago, *Homo sapiens sapiens* was widely spread throughout the warm moist regions of Africa, Europe and Asia. They did not move into North America until about 15,000 years ago, when the first settlers crossed over the frozen sea between Siberia and Alaska. They soon spread southwards, and reached the southern tip of South America by about 12,000 years ago.

People have continued to migrate in more recent times. Successive waves of people moved eastwards into Europe between 500 BC and 1000 AD. And during the last two centuries, millions of people have travelled to make a new home in the Americas.

Different races

To a biologist, a race is a large subgroup of a species that lives in a particular region and differs slightly in appearance from other subgroups. Humankind is usually described as being divided into five separate races. Nobody knows when these divisions first began.

We are all *Homo sapiens sapiens*, and there is no evidence of any variation in intelligence between the human races. But there are enormous variations in height, skin colour, and facial structure. For instance, dark skin is thought to provide better protection against strong sunlight. Each race has its own group of languages. More than 99.9 per cent of the world's population consists of people who are Caucasoid, Mongoloid or Negroid or a mixture of more than one race. Only a few people remain of the Australoid and Khoisan races.

▶ **Australoid** people have dark skins and flat noses that are suited to the hot, dry conditions of central Australia. **Caucasoid** people show the greatest variation in skin and hair colour, from the blonde-haired and fair-skinned people of northern Europe, to the dark-haired and dark-skinned people of India. **Khoisan** people, from southern Africa, have yellowish skin and their own distinctive language. **Mongoloid** people have the least body hair. Their skin colour varies. The Chinese have pale skins, the American Indians, dark skins. **Negroid** people have dark skins, and display the greatest variation in height. Both the tallest and shortest peoples of the world belong to this racial group.

The human race

Negroid

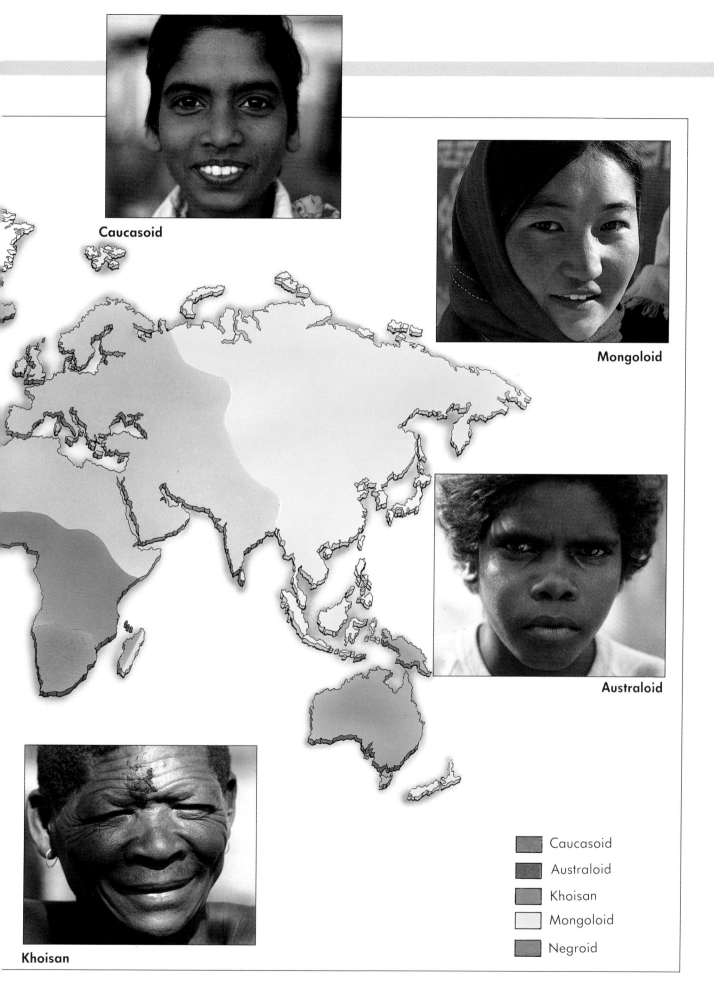

Caucasoid

Mongoloid

Australoid

Khoisan

Caucasoid
Australoid
Khoisan
Mongoloid
Negroid

31

Survival of the fittest

Spot facts

● The fossil record – the remains of early creatures found in rocks – dates from about 600 million years ago.

● The oldest species of living creature is a kind of shellfish that evolved into its present form about 550 million years ago.

● The ancestors of modern people did not appear on Earth until about 4 million years ago.

● Sabre-toothed tigers did not become extinct until 11,000 years ago.

● It takes at least 300,000 generations for a new species to evolve from an existing one.

● It is estimated that there are more than 30 million species of plants and animals on Earth today.

▶ Giraffes feeding on leaves in the treetops. According to Darwin's theory of evolution, giraffes have survived as a species because of their long necks. When food is hard to find at ground level, giraffes can continue to feed on high branches. Shorter species cannot reach this food and so they starve.

In the middle of the last century an English naturalist named Charles Darwin put forward a theory that revolutionized scientific thinking. It was a new theory of evolution, in which he tried to explain why and how life on Earth developed, or evolved in the way it did. His ideas still form the cornerstone of the modern theory of evolution. All living things, Darwin said, are locked in a continual fight for survival. Those species and individuals that are in some way better equipped for the fight tend to flourish and produce more offspring. Those that are poorly equipped tend to die out.

Darwin

Early last century, it was widely accepted that all the plant and animal species in existence had been created at the same time. The date of creation had even been calculated as 4004 BC, based on the Bible. But fossils were providing evidence of animals that no longer existed. The first dinosaur fossils were discovered in England in 1822.

In 1859 Charles Darwin challenged the accepted view of creation in one of the most important science books ever written. It had a long and rambling title: *On the Origin of Species by Means of Natural Selection, or the Preservation of Favoured Races in the Struggle for Life*. In the book, Darwin put forward the theory that life on Earth was the result of millions of years of development, or evolution.

As an idea, evolution was not new. In 1806 the Frenchman Jean-Baptiste de Lamarck had proposed that animals evolved because they tried to improve themselves. A giraffe, said Lamarck, grew its long neck by continually stretching up to reach high branches. His theory was soon replaced by Darwin's theory.

Darwin was not a trained scientist – in fact he was going to be a clergyman. But he was very interested in many different sciences, from geology to the breeding of farm animals. In 1831 he embarked on an epic five-year voyage around the world in HMS *Beagle*. It was during this voyage that he gained an insight into the processes that give rise to evolution – adaptation and natural selection. They formed the basis of his theory.

▼ Charles Darwin (left) and Alfred Russel Wallace (right). Both worked out the theory of evolution at the same time. But Darwin published first and got the credit because he had started his work earlier.

▼ Darwin and one of his "relatives", a cartoon from the *London Sketch Book* of 1874. It refers to Darwin's apparent suggestion that we were descended from monkeys. This suggestion, and indeed the whole theory of evolution, brought Darwin into conflict with many people, including the established Church. In fact, Darwin had been very careful to say nothing about human evolution in his book, because he did not want to cause offence. But this did not stop the Church's supporters from ridiculing his ideas.

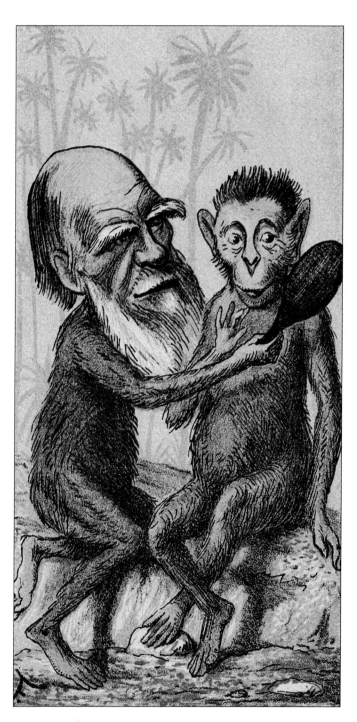

The voyage of the *Beagle*

Darwin was only 22 years old when he was appointed as the official naturalist aboard HMS *Beagle*. His main task was to collect specimens of previously undiscovered species of plants and animals and send them back to London. He carried out his duties very efficiently, but also had time to read. The latest scientific books, especially those about geology, started him thinking. But it was largely his personal observations and adventures that led to his greatest insights. Nothing in Britain had prepared him for the variety and savagery of life in the Brazilian rain forest, on the Andes Mountains or on isolated Pacific islands.

Darwin's compact microscope, an essential tool during the voyage

The numbers of the captions correspond to numbers on the map

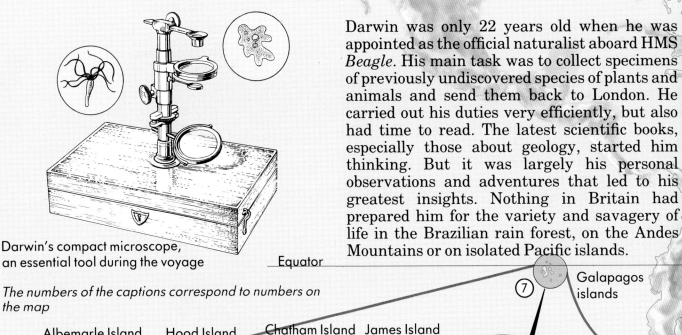

Equator

Galapagos islands

⑦

← Abingdon I.
Tower I.
Bindloe I.
Narborough I.
Equator
James I.
Indefatigable I.
Chatham I.
Albemarle I.
Charles I.
Hood I.

0°

Callao

Albemarle Island   Hood Island   Chatham Island   James Island

⑧

Galapagos giant tortoise, and shells of four island subspecies

8 In the Pacific Ocean, Darwin was able to show that atolls formed around undersea volcanoes that had risen from the ocean floor. The coral built up as the volcano slowly sank back down again.

7 Each of the Galapagos Islands had its own species of tortoise. The governor of the islands could tell them apart by the shell markings.

6 In the southern Andes Mountains Darwin witnessed a devastating earthquake, which showed Darwin how the Earth could move.

Fossil seashells found in the Andes

Corals of the Pacific and (inset) coral atoll formation

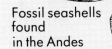

Black skimmers or scissor-beaks, observed fishing by Darwin

At La Plata in Argentina, Darwin climbed a mountain and was surprised to find fossil seashells near the summit. Later he experienced an earthquake and saw for himself how the land surface could rise, although only by a few centimetres. From this, he realized that it had taken many millions of years for a seabed to rise to the top of a mountain.

The Galapagos Islands impressed him the most. Each island had its own distinctive wildlife. This was closely related to the mainland species, but at the same time very different. How and why had this happened? The pieces of the puzzle began to fit.

▼ HMS *Beagle* set sail in December 1831. The main purpose of the voyage was to make detailed maps of the South American coast. Darwin made several long overland journeys, and met up with the ship farther down the coast. While he was away from the ship, he was free to explore and make discoveries.

HMS *Beagle*

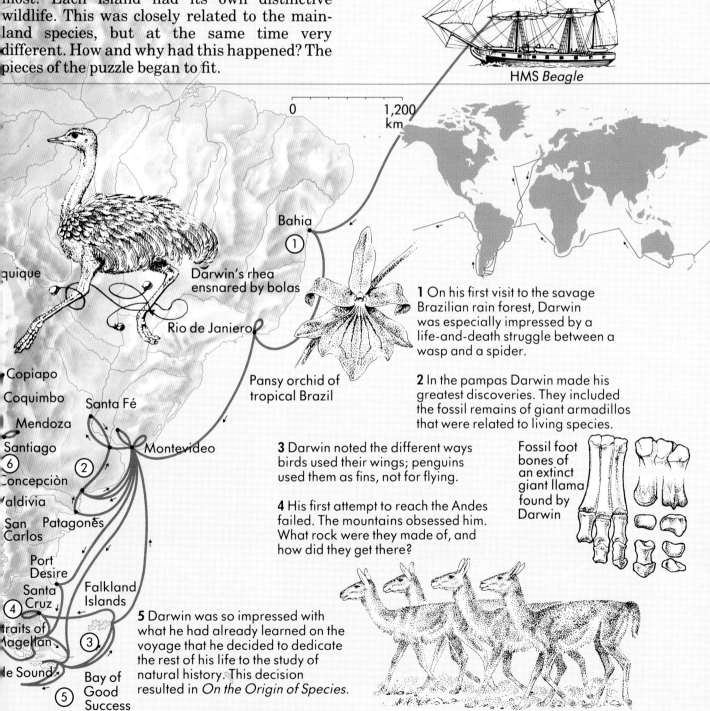

0   1,200
km

Bahia
①

Darwin's rhea
ensnared by bolas

Rio de Janiero

quique

Copiapo
Coquimbo
Mendoza   Santa Fé
Santiago
⑥   Montevideo
Concepciòn   ②
Valdivia
San   Patagonês
Carlos

Port
Desire
Santa   Falkland
Cruz   Islands
④
traits of
Magellan
③
le Sound

Bay of
⑤   Good
Success

Pansy orchid of
tropical Brazil

1 On his first visit to the savage Brazilian rain forest, Darwin was especially impressed by a life-and-death struggle between a wasp and a spider.

2 In the pampas Darwin made his greatest discoveries. They included the fossil remains of giant armadillos that were related to living species.

Fossil foot bones of an extinct giant llama found by Darwin

3 Darwin noted the different ways birds used their wings; penguins used them as fins, not for flying.

4 His first attempt to reach the Andes failed. The mountains obsessed him. What rock were they made of, and how did they get there?

5 Darwin was so impressed with what he had already learned on the voyage that he decided to dedicate the rest of his life to the study of natural history. This decision resulted in *On the Origin of Species*.

Wild llamas, or guanacos, of Patagonia

35

Adaptation

Variety, as Darwin observed, is the essence of life. Butterflies of the same species often have slightly different markings. At the same time, farmers are able to breed sheep and cattle to bring out a desirable characteristic, such as longer wool or more milk. These characteristics are then passed on to successive generations. How does this work in nature?

Life in the wild is at the mercy of the environment. In a species of millions of individuals, each new generation has some individuals with slight differences in physical form or behaviour. Many of these differences are useless, but some may prove to be an advantage. Changes that are beneficial to the species are called adaptations. Through many generations, an adaptation tends to spread throughout the species in a particular area. As a result, the species becomes well-adapted to the local environment. But the species has changed. The new characteristics mean that it has become different. In other words, it has evolved.

▼ A Giant panda feeding on its favourite food, bamboo. Its natural habitat is the foothills of the Himalayan Mountains, where bamboo is one of the commonest plants. The panda can live exclusively on bamboo. It has adapted physically for this diet by developing a sixth digit on its forepaws. This works like a thumb and enables the panda to grip the bamboo.

The more complex an organism is, the more scope there is for variation and adaptation. For example, the early shrimp-like arthropods that lived in water already had legs and eyes. They were therefore well-adapted to make the move from sea to land. Some have remained very much as they were. They still exist as scorpions. Others adapted to their new environment by evolving, over millions of years, into insects or spiders. Once crawling insects were established, some adapted further. They developed wings and took to the air.

The slow process of adaptation enables each species to find its own particular place in the great web of life. Adaptation sometimes causes what is known as convergence of form. This means that species that have similar breeding, feeding and other habits, such as sharks and dolphins, tend to look like each other. On the other hand, adaptation also causes some species to become very specialized, so that they can exist only in very special conditions.

▼ A desert grasshopper rests on the stony ground near two plants called lithops, or living stones. Both species are well camouflaged. Camouflage is a form of adaptation found widely in nature. By taking on the colours of the natural background, the grasshopper becomes much more difficult for a predator to see. And the lithops are less likely to be eaten.

▲ A dense flock of wrybills takes to the air from a seashore in New Zealand. One advantage of living in a flock is that there are many eyes available to spot predators. And if an attack does take place, the attacker will be confused by the mass of fleeing birds. So a bird in a flock has a better chance of survival than if it lived alone.

◄ This insect is a kind of mantis. It is an example of the most extreme form of adaptation. As soon as an insect lands on the "flower", it is in the insect's grasp. But the mantis is over-specialized. Without the orchid its adaptation is useless, because its strange shape and bright coloration stand out clearly against any other type of vegetation.

Natural selection

The process of evolution has been going on continuously for millions of years. We might therefore expect the world to be populated by thousands of millions of different species. But it is not. The latest estimate is about 30 million species. In other words, as evolution proceeds, many new species appear, but also many old species die out, or become extinct. What causes this to happen? What process determines whether a species survives or not? Darwin called the process natural selection.

The most important factor in the struggle for survival is the availability of food. Competition for food is usually strongest between members of related species that have similar feeding habits. Whenever food is in short supply, certain individuals may be better adapted to survive. For example, animals with a long neck can reach leaves on high branches when all the leaves on lower branches have been eaten. These animals are therefore able to survive after animals with short necks have died out. In this way, natural selection preserves any useful adaptations, such as a long neck, that may occur. Over thousands of generations these differences become established in the species and are passed on from parents to offspring.

Adaptation tends to encourage lifeforms in the same habitat to become similar in shape and behaviour. Natural selection, on the other hand, encourages the divergence of characteristics. If all organisms were the same size and ate the same food, then a single change in the environment could wipe out all life. Natural selection makes sure that there are always some forms of life able to survive.

Adaptation and natural selection form the basis of the theory of evolution. Working over millions of years, adaptation causes constant change and variety among species. At the same time, natural selection ensures that only the fittest species survive.

◀ ▼ *Hyracotherium* was the early ancestor of the horse. It lived about 50 million years ago (m.y.a.), and was the size of a small dog. It had four toes on each foot, and very simple teeth. Adaptation and natural selection have turned it into the modern horse (see chart, left).

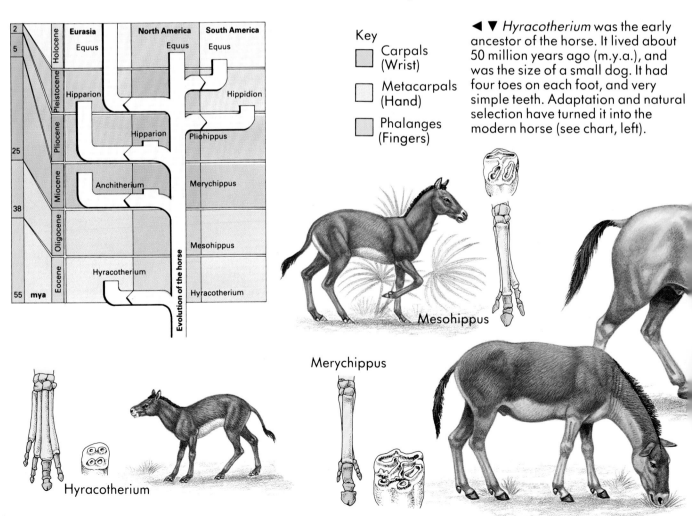

Key
- Carpals (Wrist)
- Metacarpals (Hand)
- Phalanges (Fingers)

Mesohippus

Merychippus

Hyracotherium

		Eurasia	North America	South America
2	Holocene	Equus	Equus	Equus
5	Pleistocene	Hipparion		Hippidion
	Pliocene		Hipparion	Pliohippus
25	Miocene	Anchitherium		Merychippus
38	Oligocene			Mesohippus
55 mya	Eocene	Hyracotherium		Hyracotherium

Evolution of the horse

Living fossils

In 1938 men fishing in the Indian Ocean off the coast of Africa netted a fish that had never been seen before. It was later identified as a kind of lobe-finned fish which was thought to have become extinct long ago. It was a coelacanth. A second coelacanth was caught in 1952, and since then, more than 80 have been caught. Recently, other coelacanths have been filmed in their natural deep-water habitat.

The coelacanth is a close relative of the type of fish that evolved into amphibians during the Devonian Period, about 350 million years ago. The discovery of the coelacanth was a reminder of just how incomplete the fossil record is.

▶ This is a fossil of *Hyracotherium*, the ancestor of the horse. Over a period of 50 million years, the horse has grown progressively larger. Its feet have gradually evolved from having four toes to only one, because a single hoof on each foot is better for galloping at speed over open grassland. Also, the ridges on the surface of the teeth have become much more complex. The ridges make the teeth much more efficient at grinding up grass.

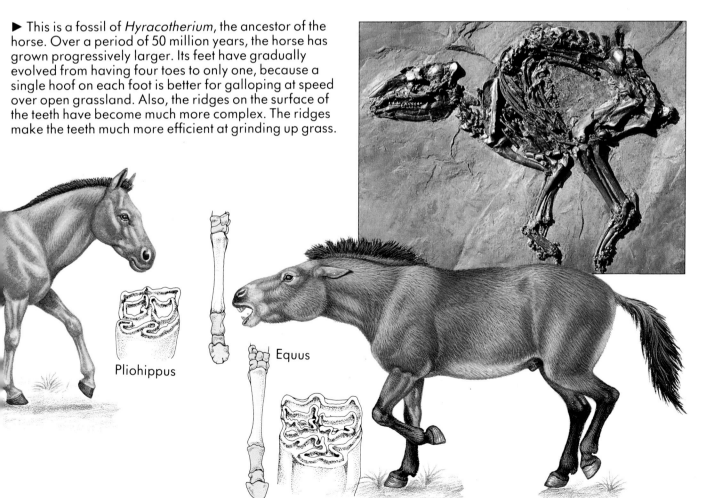

Pliohippus

Equus

Evolution in action

The theory of evolution explains why living things developed the way they did. It is almost certain that plants developed first, and that the first multi-celled animals were herbivores, or plant-eaters. Meat-eating animals, or carnivores, developed much later, when there were enough herbivores for them to feed on. Depending on the animals concerned, it takes 20 to 100 herbivores to support one carnivore. For example, a lion that feeds once a week must kill and eat 52 animals every year.

Adaptation is constantly producing new types of herbivore, which are more efficient at feeding on the available vegetation. At the same time, new forms of carnivore are developing, which have to compete with each other to feed on the available prey animals. In both cases, natural selection produces specialists and generalists. Specialists are animals that feed on one particular type of plant or animal. Generalists are animals that are much less choosy about their food.

Varieties of marsupials. Marsupials are mammals that raise their young in a pouch. They evolved separately from other mammals. Yet adaptation to similar habitats has produced similar body forms in marsupials and other mammals. The wolf (1a) and marsupial wolf (1b) are medium-sized predators. The wood mouse (2a) and marsupial mulgara (2b) are small scavengers. The Californian mole (3a) and marsupial mole (3b) both live underground.

◀ Dark and light forms of the Peppered moth on a soot-covered tree. The Peppered moth originally had a pale, speckled appearance. This camouflaged it from predators while it was resting on a tree branch. During the Industrial Revolution, smoke and soot turned many trees almost black with pollution. As a result, the Peppered moth developed a much darker coloration, which provided much better camouflage in the new conditions.

This new form of the moth remained confined to industrial areas. In country areas, far away from industrial cities, the moth still kept its paler markings. Now that the industrial nations are starting to control air pollution, the darker varieties of moth will probably adapt back to their original colour.

Predators and prey

The relationship between animals that hunt (predators) and animals that are hunted (prey) has caused some of the most interesting of all adaptations. Usually, prey animals rely on speed to escape from predators. But sometimes evolution takes a different course. The struggle for survival becomes a straight battle between attack and defence.

This evolutionary "arms race" was notable when dinosaurs ruled the Earth. Despite its fearsome appearance, the 5-tonne *Triceratops* (below left) was a placid herbivore. The armoured neck frill and razor sharp horns were purely for defence. *Triceratops* evolved such massive protection because it shared its habitat with some very fierce predators. *Tyrannosaurus* (below right), for example, was superbly equipped as a hunter. It had a massive head and powerful jaws.

But it probably left *Triceratops* well alone, because the chances of a successful attack were greatly outweighed by the risk of serious injury.

Evolution and the changing Earth

During the time life has flourished on Earth, the shape of the Earth's surface has changed completely. The change has been brought about by continental drift. This is the very gradual movement of plates, or sections, of the Earth's crust. In the Cambrian Period there were only four continents. They were not the continents we know today, and they were in very different positions. Gradually they drifted together. By the time of the Devonian Period there were only three continents.

By the Permian Period, all the continents had come together to form one super-continent, known as Pangaea. By the middle of the Cretaceous Period, the present-day continents were drifting apart. During the Tertiary Period they moved towards their present positions. By about 40,000 years ago, the world was almost exactly as we know it today. Yet the continents are still moving very slowly. In 100 million years time the world will again look different.

The drifting of the continents and other changes in the land masses made the sea level rise and fall. While life remained in the seas, changes in sea level made little difference to evolution. But once life had moved on to the land, the changes in sea level started to affect the course of evolution. For example, during the Devonian Period, the sea level was very low and drought was widespread. But during the following Carboniferous Period, the sea level was much higher. This caused the swampy and humid conditions in which giant forests and amphibians thrived.

Later, the various land masses became separated. This allowed evolution to continue in isolation. During the last 5 million years, ice ages have also affected the distribution of animals. For example, they caused bridges of frozen sea to form between Asia and North America. Animals migrated between the two continents across the bridges.

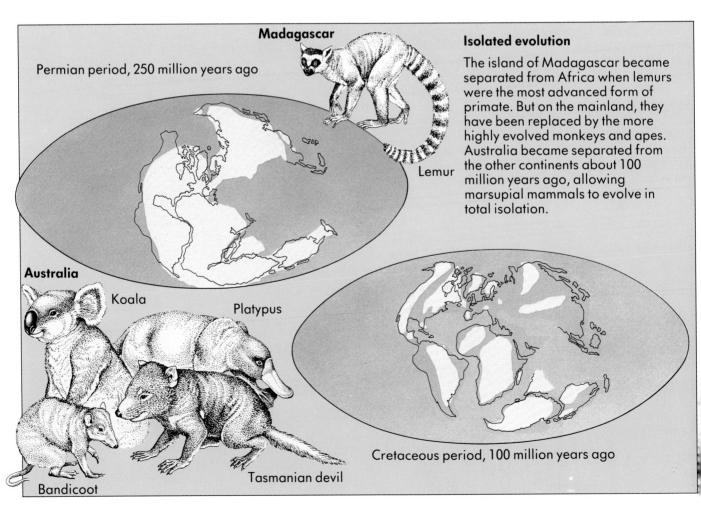

Madagascar

Permian period, 250 million years ago

Lemur

Isolated evolution

The island of Madagascar became separated from Africa when lemurs were the most advanced form of primate. But on the mainland, they have been replaced by the more highly evolved monkeys and apes. Australia became separated from the other continents about 100 million years ago, allowing marsupial mammals to evolve in total isolation.

Australia

Koala

Platypus

Cretaceous period, 100 million years ago

Tasmanian devil

Bandicoot

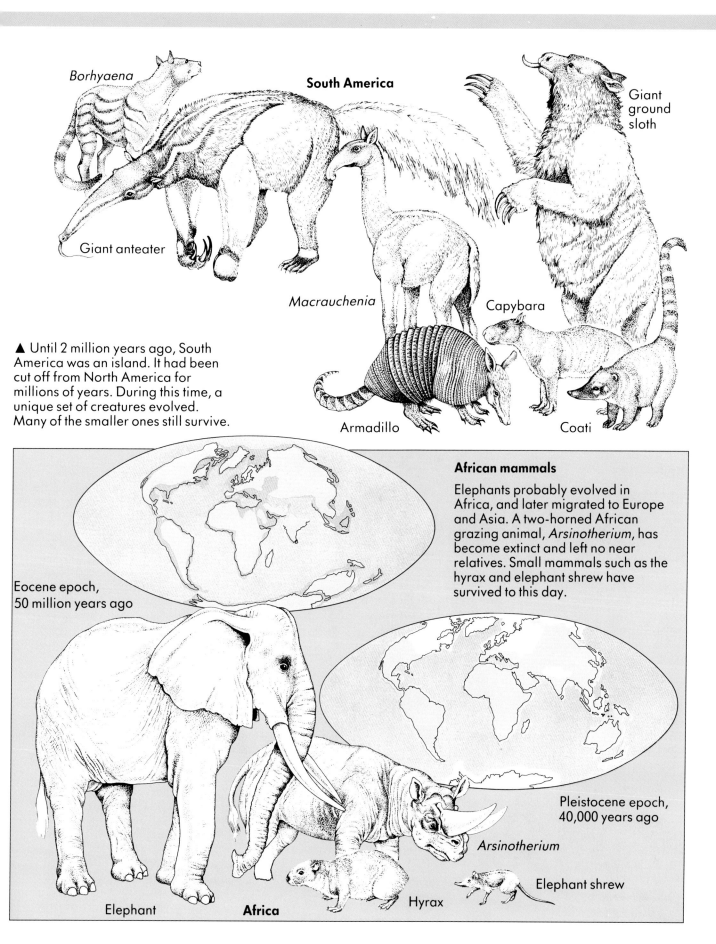

Borhyaena

South America

Giant
ground
sloth

Giant anteater

Macrauchenia

Capybara

▲ Until 2 million years ago, South America was an island. It had been cut off from North America for millions of years. During this time, a unique set of creatures evolved. Many of the smaller ones still survive.

Armadillo

Coati

Eocene epoch,
50 million years ago

African mammals

Elephants probably evolved in Africa, and later migrated to Europe and Asia. A two-horned African grazing animal, *Arsinotherium*, has become extinct and left no near relatives. Small mammals such as the hyrax and elephant shrew have survived to this day.

Pleistocene epoch,
40,000 years ago

Arsinotherium

Elephant shrew

Elephant

Africa

Hyrax

43

Glossary

adaptation The process by which the characteristics of a species gradually change in response to the environment. The term can also refer to a particular characteristic.

algae The group of primitive plants that includes single-celled plants and seaweeds. Some algae cannot photosynthesize and are closely related to bacteria.

amino acid One of a group of complex organic molecules that can link together to form proteins. They are considered to be the building blocks of life.

amphibians A group of animals that evolved after the fishes. Young amphibians live in water and have gills, adults breath air through lungs.

arthropods A group of animals with a hard external skeleton and jointed limbs. It includes crustaceans, insects and the extinct trilobites.

Australopithecus An early hominid. The word means "southern ape".

bacteria A group of micro-organisms, neither animals nor plants. They are the smallest and most primitive form of life.

biology The science of life. Different branches of study are concerned with the structure, functions, organization and distribution of living things.

Cambrian Period The period about 590-505 million years ago, when life began to flourish in abundance.

Carboniferous Period The period about 360-286 million years ago, during which most coal seams were laid down.

carnivore Any animal that obtains its food by eating other animals. A few plants that absorb trapped insects are also described as carniverous.

Cenozoic Era The era of recent life, which began about 65 million years ago; it includes the Tertiary and Quaternary Periods.

Cretaceous Period The period about 144-65 million years ago, during which most chalk beds were laid down.

crustaceans A group of arthropods, which includes woodlice and crabs.

Darwinian theory The theory of evolution, as put forward by Darwin.

Devonian Period The period about 408-360 million years ago, which saw the evolution of many kinds of fishes and amphibians.

dinosaurs A group of animals that flourished on Earth between 200-65 million years ago. Some were huge armoured monsters, others were no bigger than a small dog.

Eocene Epoch The time that saw the "dawn" of recent life, that is, the rise of modern species, about 55-38 million years ago.

epoch An interval of geological time, shorter than a period, in the Cenozoic Era.

era An interval of geological time, which is divided into periods. The three eras are Palaeozoic, Mesozoic and Cenozoic.

eukaryote A complex cell containing a nucleus and other specialized structures. Virtually all forms of life are composed of eukaryotic cells.

evolution The generally accepted theory that life on Earth began in very simple forms that have slowly developed into the more complex forms.

extinction The complete elimination of a living species. There have been mass extinctions – extinctions of many species at the same time – at various times in the Earth's history.

fossil Any physical evidence, even footprints, of ancient life. Most fossils are found in rocks, and have been formed by an organism becoming buried in mud and gradually turning to stone.

genus A subdivision in the classification of living things below family and above species.

geological timescale The splitting up of geological time into intervals, separated from one another by major changes in rock types or layers, or sudden changes in the fossil groups found within the layers. Major divisions are era, period and epoch.

geology The science of the structure of the Earth. By examining rock samples, geologists have been able to explain how the Earth was formed and how the continents have moved.

habitat Natural surroundings in which a particular plant or animal exists. The term is much more specific and localized than the environment.

hand-axe A well-crafted stone tool used by prehistoric people for various cutting purposes.

herbivore Any animal that eats only plants. The first animals were all herbivores; carnivores could only evolve once there were enough herbivores for them to eat.

Holocene epoch The most recent epoch, beginning about 10,000 years ago.

hominid Belonging to the same group of animals as humans. The term is usually applied to humans' early ancestors which we know only from fossil evidence.

Homo The genus to which modern people and our immediate ancestors belong. We are genus *Homo*, species *sapiens*, subspecies *sapiens*.

ice ages Times when glaciers covered very much larger areas of the Earth than they do at present.

invertebrate Any animal that does not have an internal skeleton centered on the backbone. Insects, spiders, worms and shellfish are all invertebrates.

Jurassic Period The period about 213-144 million years ago, during which birds evolved.

Lamarckism An idea of evolution proposed by Lamarck, who suggested that animals developed as they tried to improve themselves.

mammals A group of animals that are warm-blooded and give birth to live young, which are suckled on the mother's milk. Dogs, cats, mice and humans are all mammals.

marsupial A type of primitive mammal in which the young are born live, but are then carried in the mother's pouch where they continue to develop.

Mesozoic Era The era of middle life, about 248-65 million years ago. It was the age of the reptiles.

migration A large-scale movement of a species, usually over great distances. The movement may be temporary (e.g. seasonal) or permanent.

Miocene Epoch An epoch of the Tertiary Period, about 25-5 million years ago, in which higher apes evolved.

natural selection The process in evolution that determines which adaptations are preserved and which are allowed to die out. In general, natural selection favours the survival of the fittest.

Neanderthal people A group of hominids, related to modern people, that died out about 35,000 years ago. Neanderthals were, like modern people a subspecies of *Homo sapiens* ("wise man").

nucleus A small dark area found in virtually all living cells. The nucleus normally stores the cell's DNA, and controls the operation of the various organelles inside the cell.

Oligocene Epoch An epoch of the Tertiary Period, about 38-25 million years ago.

Ordovician Period The period about 505-438 million years ago, during which jawless fish appeared.

Palaeocene Epoch The epoch of ancient life, about 65-55 million years ago; first epoch of the Tertiary Period.

Palaeontology The study of fossils.

Palaeozoic Era The era of ancient life, about 590-248 milliion years ago.

period An interval of geological time, shorter than an era, and longer than an epoch.

Permian Period The period about 286-248 million years ago, marked by the expansion of the reptiles.

photosynthesis The process by which nearly all plants can use sunlight to turn water and carbon dioxide into food.

Pleistocene Epoch The early epoch of the Quaternary Period about 2 million- 10,000 years ago.

Pliocene Epoch The last epoch of the Tertiary Period, 5-2 million years ago.

predator Any animal that actively hunts other animals (known as prey) for food. Most carnivores are also predators.

prehistoric The term that describes anything that existed or occurred more than about 10,000 years ago. Dinosaurs and cave-people are both considered prehistoric although they are separated by about 65 million years.

primates The group of mammals that are considered to be the most highly evolved animals. Monkeys, apes and humans are all primates.

prokaryote The primitive form of cell that lacks a central nucleus. Today the only prokaryotes are bacteria.

protozoa The collective term for all microscopic, single-celled animals.

Quaternary Period The most recent period of geological time, beginning about 2 million years ago, marked by the emergence of modern people.

reptiles The group of cold-blooded animals that breathe air through lungs at all stages of their life. Lizards, snakes and crocodiles are all reptiles.

sediment Material transported by flowing water and deposited, for example, in the sea. Rocks formed from sediments – sedimentary rocks – are the source of most fossils.

Silurian Period The period about 438-408 million years ago, during which the first land plants became established.

species The most precise form of grouping of a type of plant or animal. All members of the same species have the same characteristics and differ only slightly in size or markings.

Tertiary Period The period about 65-2 million years ago, notable for the rise of the mammals.

Triassic Period The period about 248-213 million years ago, which saw the expansion of the dinosaurs and the emergence of the mammals.

trilobite One of the most successful early invertebrate animals that looked somewhat like a woodlouse. Trilobites thrived about 590-260 million years ago.

vertebrate Any animal that has a backbone and internal skeleton. All the advanced animals, from fishes to primates, are vertebrates.

Index

Page numbers in *italics* refer to pictures.

Further Reading

Discovering Life on Earth by David Attenborough (Collins, 1989)
The Story of Life On Earth by Michael Benton, (Kingfisher, 1986)
The Young Scientist's Book of Evolution by L. Bresler and B. Cork (Usborne, 1985)
Dinodots by Dougal Dixon (Eddison-Sadd, 1988)
Prehistoric Life (Just Look at Series) by Richard Moody (Macdonald, 1984)
Dinosaurs and How They Lived by Steve Parker (Dorling Kindersley, 1989)